On the Theory of Unnatural Unnaturalness Becoming Natural Unnaturalness

On the Theory of Unnatural Unnaturalness Becoming Natural Unnaturalness

◆

An Analysis through Poetics (That Which Would Prove the Existence of a *Beyond*, if Architecture=Denotation)

Mihajlo Bugarinovic

iUniverse, Inc.
New York Lincoln Shanghai

On the Theory of Unnatural Unnaturalness Becoming Natural Unnaturalness

An Analysis through Poetics (That Which Would Prove the Existence of a *Beyond*, if Architecture=Denotation)

iUniverse books may be ordered through booksellers or by contacting:

iUniverse
2021 Pine Lake Road, Suite 100
Lincoln, NE 68512
www.iuniverse.com
1-800-Authors (1-800-288-4677)

ISBN-13: 978-0-595-35485-6 (pbk)
ISBN-13: 978-0-595-79977-0 (ebk)
ISBN-10: 0-595-35485-8 (pbk)
ISBN-10: 0-595-79977-9 (ebk)

Printed in the United States of America

Contents

Preface

The validity of the unpretentiousness in the instance of a forfeit, not preventing the suffering of *microcosm* to prevent *macrocosm*, proving the theoretically proved moral values' practical worth, balance *vs.* anti-balance and (*as oppose to*) natural chaos *vs.* unnatural chaos, in short, what this book is about.

The internality of the perfectly balanced, is that not the ultimate goal, the ultimate achievement ambushing our unsuppressed state of natural unnaturalness' natural chaos? Natural unnaturalness is the root of everything when one considers unnatural unnaturalness to be the result of this ambush, not the source: being derived from natural unnaturalness by the ways of shame, and intrinsic guilt, for that which is at its most natural when guilty.

Yes, organizing guilt into "non-guilty" and "guilty," organizing that which is guilty by its nature into that which it is not, is the most elevated form of guilt. Yes, that would mean that he who has stated the previous "yes" and this "yes" believes in chaos. For he understands that the only way to prevent chaos is to accept chaos: natural chaos vs. unnatural chaos, balance vs. anti-balance, natural unnaturalness vs. unnatural unnaturalness-these conflicts are all sourced in natural chaos. The third "yes," the working backward toward that which has worked its way forward, has so far only been integrated into the reality of the suppression.

This suppression, which some epitomize as being represented by ideals, is a far broader term than it may seem, one that is the producer of ideals, not synonymous with. For when a philosopher comes along and creates a persona for himself that suppresses his nature of a suppressed nature, and therefore criticizes what he has suppressed as if he has successfully worked back toward what he is criticizing, the way to sum it up, and thus the man, is with a realization that provides us with an idea of the suppression of a suppressed nature's results: writing aphorisms that are like an invisible magnifying glass for communicating a writer's inability to eliminate the idea that aphorisms should be interpreted literally.

No, ideals are not the suppression's synonym; it is the way these ideals have been communicated through appalling organizational forces, and the very fact that they were communicated. No, it is the anhelation, not the oxygen. The oxygen's purity results in a slow, glorious death as inhalation is defectively deceptive while being at the same time deceptively defective (glorious because, just like every death, life is born out of it). Thus, the third "no," "This slow death is unpreventable," would be going against the "*a posteriori.*" It not taking place would be going against its nature.

The pastiche-like qualities that the oxygen assumes because of the prolonged complexion given to the anhelation by its failed inhalator, they are exactly what the ambushed natural unnaturalness amounts to: emitting becoming inhaling of emitting through the extermination of inhaling being the emitter of inhaling, an initially contradictory nature of the role of the inhalation and the exhalation that gave way to a one-layered contradiction's idea of the oxygen being visible and being the oxygen at the same time. Of course, there is no proof that the oxygen is invisible apart from the fact that it is oxygen. The question is, the pastiche-like qualities that the oxygen assumes because of the prolonged complexion given to the anhelation, are they pastiche-like in the eyes of the *cured,* or in the eyes of that which never had a need to be cured?

Aphorisms on the Morality of Pretentiousness

1

The choice of either suppressing or letting loose the internality emblematic of nihilism does not exist under the pressures of nihilistic realizations.

2

Supporting chaos to prevent chaos belongs to: one *should* strive for moral immorality to prevent immoral immorality.

3

I do not hate humans. I hate that they hate themselves, and thus do not.

4

Just because a source is a root of destruction, it does not imply that it in itself believes in construction.

5

Nihilism=anti-foundationalism: the impotence of women, the menopause of men.

6

That a piece of music is conceived intellectually does not embody how it should be played.

7

Receiving goodness under the condition of not exceeding its source is the most gangrenous form of slavery.

8

For a decayed tooth to be replaced by a new one, it has to be decayed.

9

A motif for the influenced under nihilism: the morphing of suffering=ability to *love* into suffering=ability to feel nothing (which in some cases leads to hate).

10

Assuming the state of anti-snobbishness is the highest snobbishness.

11

By demonstrating goodness received as an act that is owed to, disrespect to the giver is signified, representation of the gift as an outward expression of a dislike.

12

Respect for the old should not be treating them as if they are old.

13

Only an idealist has the potential of becoming nihilism's representative.

14

It is inescapable to conclude that post-nihilism *is* a Brahms symphony.

On Civilization

The Meeting between the <u>Real</u> and the <u>Apparent</u> Worlds in the Context of the Paradox of Pre-Nihilism as the Root of Nihilism, and Nihilism as the Root of its Root

The *Unnaturalness* of a Heat-Resistant Glass

The *unnaturalness* of a heat-resistant glass,
In the form of crushing clodhoppers will pass,
The sadness, transformation into opaque,
Gloriously, without an intolerant shack.

Obeisance of the closure of cloddishness,
It obeys bigamy's childishness,
Amblyopsis' golden medal amblyopia,
Its transparency shall rot away to hyperopia.

The nucleus demonstrated through half-blindness,
Scarily blinded in its half-highness,
Its foundation found on the firmness of blindness,
It is rooted in the half-blindness of shyness.

Timidness' pretentious pretentiousness for ophthalmia,
Amphibiousness' pretentious unpretentiousness for anaerobia,
Their relationship of *a* creator and the creator,
Created the unnaturalness of the burned fuel as *a* peat's realtor.

A creator of the creator,
He is not a creator of the creator's predator,
Of *a* creator's creation,
The appraisal of the creator's creator as an occupation.

A creator of *a* creator's creation,
He is not a creator of *a* creator's ornamentation,
Of the creator's patrimony,
The labyrinthine contradictions of a ceremony.

A creator of the creator's creation,
He who will provide the creator with a pension,
Of *a* creator he is a creator,
But is not *a* creator's mentor.

Timidness' sterilization is a shark's creator,
A creator of a predator's translator,
Of a camber's dual inclinator,
Angelfish's division inflator.

The nucleus' role being a camber,
It proves the timelessness of an omnipotent clamber,
The blind half-blindness' underlying pate,
A base, it is a nuance's chateau.

Obeisance of a camber's union,
Lost angelfish's passive disunion,
Through the art of a bloody communion,
Will be disunited with its disunion.

The *unnaturalness* of a heat-resistant glass,
In the form of crushing clodhoppers will pass,
The sadness, transformation into opaque,
Gloriously, without an intolerant shack.

The *Unnaturalness* of a Heat-Resistant Glass II:

Actinism's *Inverted*

It places itself, the radiantly, like an opaque glass handled
by itself and puttied by the not itself,
in the control of the timing lacking's,
inverting its purpose by burning off a tumor,
creating two of what it burned, so that
it can burn more, always by one,
eventually gets itself melted from its own,
the sun's heat from the puttied's unseen,
having its liquid freshly formulated,
hardened into the heat-resistant
by the not its own.

The new transparency's four edges,
seen as well,
being placed into a transparent frame
allowed for the quadraphonic to be
prickling-proof at last.

The accepted state of the tumor-suffering
and the early death thereof,
the opaque's was not broken
transitioned into the transparency's *looked through,*
this long-faced monkey with cheeks
hanging the in its pouches,
did not know its potentials,
finally swallowed and threw out.

The *Unnaturalness* of a Heat-Resistant Glass III:

The Shark's Skeleton Talking

I was a very odd shark. Out a total lack of reason,
I always chased what was beneath the surface. I had a will
of a whale, and a skin of a shark.

Fish were the only food I would ever think of consuming.
I chased them arrogantly, their massive accumulations,
from time to time visiting the surface with people screaming
around me without reason, until on one occasion a group of
fishes escaped my jaws and went underneath me. There they
found something that even I did not expect them to find, a
zipper.

One of them saw itself as the leader of this little group, and
with its little opening for food took the tab and slid it all the
way, from my head to my tail. My skeleton, I, slid down to the
bottom of the sea as there was no cushioning inside this skin,
no meat, except an artificial lining. The leader of the group
called more of its kind, and they all entered my sharkskin,
closed the zipper, and went off.

And that's how it came to my having a conversation with you,
here, at the bottom of the sea.

A *<u>Beyond</u>* as an Allegory

An Oasis inside a Closet

A philosopher-poet would have us believe:

Inclination of their conversation is bier,
One that holds pope's monastery,
Like a happy tune of a lyre,
How is it that we have reached unnatural unnaturalness,
When our goal has always been that of finesse.

Aside from the *event of the future*, he would be right.

The future's *What I would have us believe*:

Bilaterally secreted out of an ancient shell,
He "entered" the world of a photoelectric cell,
Source of extermination is,
Was a rower,
Whose pledge was the opposite of a grenade thrower.

In the eyes of "this" "'trailblazing'" dwell,
The peddler is a dwarf,
Wearing the clothes of a resounding to-knell,
A pygmy seemingly stalled,
Teary, he does not want to be hauled.

"This" light measurer, it contains outcasts,
Those pretentiously bifurcated musical rests,
Giving hope to an invisible closet,
A failed clone with a purpose to abdicate.

A loud lament was horned,
An oasis inside a closet, formed,
The dwarf, his chests spreading the horizon,
Fixed the pedal, and oared like a gigantic "wizen."

The music of the "crest,"
A keepsake inside an empty chest,
It is the creator of a paradise,
One waiting to break through its invisible disguise.

The Designation of *Belonging*

The Imprint of the Reflection

In order for the *homeless,*
to become the *homeless,*
once again,
the imprint of the reflection
needs to become a reality.

In order for the *homelessness,*
to become the *homelessness,*
once again,
the imprint of an old
needs to become a reality.

In order for *an old,*
to become *an old,*
once again,
the imprint of its *opposite*
needs to become a reality.

In order for the *reflection,*
to become the *reflection,*
once again,
a mirror reflecting the unnatural unnaturalness
needs to become a reality.

In order for the anomalistic,
to become the *anomalistic,*
once again,
a mirror reflecting the perfectly balanced
needs to become a reality.

In order for *a full circle,*
to become a full circle,
once again,
a mirror reflecting the natural unnaturalness
needs to become a reality.

In order for the *natural unnaturalness,*
to become the natural unnaturalness,
once again,
the imprint of the perfectly unbalanced
needs to become a reality.

Will the possibility of the
physical demonstration
of an old reflection
striving for the old

source's new
reflection
become a
reality? (If the execution of the old source does take place, that is.)

The Imprint of the Reflection II:

A New, Perfect Creator

In terms of unaware of the shakiness' source,
Caffeine as a delayed realizations' remorse,
The conclusion of consumers' endeavors,
May come in the shape of their achieving,
a *new, perfect creator's* compound levers.

Just like the old *root* of hates,
This new, perfect creates,
Would then be an opening,
A possibility for the concept "mates,"
Working backward, toward the old, creates.

Rejection as a means,
As a providing oneself,
With its opposing hymns,
Is such a carefully designed in the world of schemes,
It would evaporate the definable of Him's.

On Asses

The Plum's Disintegration

What the *plum* had to say:

Whether or not prunes are fulfilling
is a question of taste. However, once
the realization of what kind of a sun
they were dried under becomes
apparent, this question of taste
ceases to exist.

For this sun is not the true source of light,
but a one that uses the true source in
order to create for itself the role of that
which it is not.

What the plum had to say:

I got very disappointed
when I
realized that none
of these prune-lovers wanted to eat me
before I became a prune.
Now that some people find me tasteful, I am curious as to why everyone objects
to my being dried to extinction, prune's becoming a plum again under
the same
sun that sculpted it
into a prune.

The fact is,
I failed to realize that by becoming a prune
I exterminated my creator.
And even though no one
is aware of the awareness that
the new
sun is not an impostor,
everyone is now using this true source of light

in creating
roles for themselves (roles that they are unaware of having).

Which is the plum, the *plum* or *I*?

The Plum's Disintegration II:

Two Streams

The process of the plum's disintegration, with its starting point halfway through the first side of the triangular nature of it, is associable with an image of two streams running one on top of the other, the upper one acting as the source of the pressure to the lower one. The illusionary function of the presser is that of clotting, a solidification into an object that seems to float aimlessly on top of the lower stream, but in reality has the function of uniting the upper and the lower streams through the process of it being liquidated once again.

The Plum's Disintegration III:

The Russian Doll's Disintegration
(An Analogy of
Rhythm *vs.* Chaos)

What the *plum* had to say:

The giant hand discovered that the agoraphobia
of the Russian doll's, its inside's, the child, was no longer there.
The unobtrusive nature of it can only be fully
explained by its a behind-the-curtain, the behind a large
kakemono, as a play.

What happened in this, the greatest of them all, the play?

As the grasping's descended upon the doll,
it grasped to reveal of the ungraspable's.
As the logic behind each layer, its of
presented the fall, did show a new of the
definition to the dol.
A vertical dissection through the middle
would have explained the hollowness's' externalities as hollow,
reasoned the slight inconvenience, that is, of, indeed, being shallow,
except the solidness, its child's the inner.
The hand closed the doll, firstly,
the moment it found inner most was stretching
to become outer, momentary relief
did not last very long, the shout, smallest grew
to a popping, its as a drought's, the mostly.

What happened in this, the greatest of them all, the drought?

The giant hand discovered that the agoraphobia
of the Russian doll's, its inside's, the child, was no longer there.
The unobtrusive nature of it can only be fully
explained by its a behind-the-curtain, the behind a large
kakemono, as a play.

Epilogue

After the balloons were
popped one by one, and the
baby grew up to be
a solid clone that did
eventually shrink
back to original
size, large kakemono
was used as a screen for
projecting what happened
in behind-the-curtain.

What the plum had to say:

The giant hand discovered that the agoraphobia
of the Russian doll's insides was no longer there.
The unobtrusive nature of it can only be explained
by its behind-the-curtain, behind a large kakemono,
as a play.

What happened in this, the greatest of them all, the play?

As the grasping's descended upon the doll,
it grasped to reveal the ungraspable's.
As the logic behind each layer presented the fall,
It showed a new definition's to the dol.

A vertical dissection through the middle's the callow
would have showed the hollowness's' the hollow,
reasoned the slight inconvenience of being shallow,
that is, except the solidness of the child's the mallow.

The hand's closed the doll the moment it found out.
Its momentary relief lasted short, the shout.
The inner most's was expanding to become the outer most's,
the smallest grew, stretching to a popping as a drought.

What happened in this, the greatest of them all, the drought?

The giant hand discovered that the agoraphobia
of the Russian doll's insides was no longer there.
The unobtrusive nature of it can only be explained
by its behind-the-curtain, behind a large kakemono,
as a play.

Epilogue

After the balloons were popped one by one,
the baby grown up to become a solid clone
that eventually shrunk back to its original size,
the large kakemono was used as a screen for
projecting a film of what happened in its
behind-the-curtain.

Which is the plum, the *plum* or *I*?

The Plum's Disintegration IV:

The Stone's: Macadam's Substitute

A scientist once pondered:
Is there function's essence's function?
He took the giant plum's stone, grinded it through a machine
he invented, and used it as a substitute for macadam, making
a road, and waiting in the middle to see who would travel it.

He looked to the right of his hand used for noting down
the results, and from a distance, it looked like an ordinary bicycle,
nothing more. He wrote this down, started packing to leave, and
tried to put a smile on his face when all of a sudden he no longer
had to try. As the bicycle advanced its route towards its observer,
it revealed a follower, or rather, a carriage.

None of his *a posteriori* or *a priori* knowledge prepared him for
what he was about to experience, what he was about to not experience.
When the bizarre appearance found itself close to the middle
of the road, it finally revealed the face of its cyclist, an ancient-looking
man with a beard and hair the length of his body. It was still unclear,
at this point, what was to be found on the carriage.

The facial features of the carrier were most unusual, conveying a very strange
image to its scientist. The nose was big, to say the least, and seemed to be pointed
more downward than upward. It had a layer of scar tissue, little holes that could
only be explained by a past soaked in suffering from either black spots that were
once
forced out violently, or pimples that had their share of internal buildup, again,
forced out, violently. This *theory* was strongly supported by the factuality of the
rest of
his face being populated by a pimply colony waiting to be ruptured. The eye-
brows
matched this colony perfectly, with the outer edges pointing downward and the
inner

ones upward, wrinkling the middle of his forehead, making an unstable
terrain for its population. The lower part of his face, including the mouth, the
chin,
and the cheeks, was all covered in facial hair, completely indistinguishable.

The first thing the scientist noticed about this strange man was that there seemed
to be
blood running down his beard and his hair. The only logical conclusion he could
come up
with was that some of it was pulled out. He looked around to find the source, and
noticed that it probably had something to do with the hair curled-up around the
thin, metal spikes
not usually found on a wheel of a bicycle. Since the stranger's hair was long
enough to be dragged
on the ground, it was probably caught up, and found a new purpose.

At first, he thought that maybe he should share his observations with the
observed, but then realized it would not be very courteous.

"Lovely day," he said, trying to find a way to start a conversation.

"A bit painful, but yes, lovely."

"Sorry?"

"A bit painful, but lovely."

There is a pause.

"I am sorry, but for some reason I am having a hard time hearing you."

"I said, a bit painful, but lovely nevertheless!"

The conversation didn't start well, and the scientist decided to apologize, in a
subtle way of course.

"I seem to be having hearing problems lately. I should have my ears checked as
soon as possible."

"No worries. I know how physical defects can sometimes get in the way when being around other people."

The scientist could not hear a single word, but decided that from now on he will pretend that he can hear everything perfectly, by having a smile on his face, a smile that would correspond to every emotional nuance.

After about five minutes of this useless *exchange* of opinions, he concluded that he has to find some
way of letting the old man know that he can get rid of the pain. Then, he remembered that he had a pair of small scissors in his pocket. Pretending as if he is shuffling through it aimlessly, he pulled the scissors out and put a face of surprise on his face.

The old man said something immediately, and judging by the sparks in his eyes, the scientist knew that he wanted the scissors, badly. Instead of giving them to him, he resolved to cut the extraneous hair himself.

His assumption of being a hairstylist all of a sudden proved catastrophic. For the face of his "*friend*"
turned out to be so ugly he could no longer contain himself:

"My God, you are the ugliest man I have ever seen."

Once he said it, he regretted it. However, it turned out to be too late to recover their *relationship*, and the old man got ready to leave insulted and filled with rage.

The scientist tried to smooth things out one last time, and using his experiences as a dermatologist,
gave the desperate man some cream. The shaved man threw it on the ground and as he was leaving, the scientist asked one last thing.

"Why do you go on cycling when you are on the verge of being dead? I mean, yes, your skin is not exactly perfect, but it's not going to get better with all the sweat that you are soaked in. Don't you realize this sweat is feeding off itself? Don't you know that the dirt under your skin, the sweat that couldn't get out, is what causes you to have bad skin? Why do you go on, why?"

"It is God's will."

As always, it was too whispery to be heard by anyone, but this time the scientist was able to read the lips, the lips of what he thought, of what he was sure of, now, was an unintelligent man.

"God didn't create this road, I did," he answered turning his back and getting packed to depart.
He took the sticky, full-of-old-blood hair, making it ready for further analysis, and as he took his first steps toward his lab, he realized that he missed something very important in his observations. What was hiding in the carriage? He turned around to face the bizarre reality one, last time, and saw something that made the "bizarre" useless, and that finally revealed the true purpose of his road.

His notebook states:

In conclusion of my experiment, I have come to believe that the mere fact that I ran it proves
the existence of the function's essence's function. The experiment began not after its purpose has been stated, but before.

It was an old man on a bicycle attached to a kabuki theater that sensed my road as useful.
By using my scientific knowledge I have constructed a road for the unexplainable, and ultimately scientifically impossible. A group of actors, male, were performing their act, while one man with complexes beyond our grasp, one ugly man, soaked in sweat and with blood running down his whole self transported an entire theater across my road.

Just because a scientist builds the road, it does not mean that some kind of a beyond did not have a hand in it.

The Naturalness of Natural Unnaturalness Becoming Unnatural Unnaturalness

Pruning

Should it be eliminated, the control over the means of producing that which pertains to the properties of psychedelic?

Pruning is an
act of immorality,
thus morality. The control over the means
of producing that which pertains to the properties
of psychedelic does need to be in existence for the natural arc of natural
unnaturalness going to unnatural unnaturalness and then back to natural unnaturalness to take place.

Idealism within Autonomy, and Autonomy's <u>vice</u> as Prohibited for a Selected Few

Fugue's Constant

To what extent does the phrasal structure of a fugue subject have the right to remain unchanged?

It exists only in a surrounding supportive of the inclusion of a beyond, caesural beyond.

To what extent does the phrasal structure of a kneeling's knuckle's Marrow have the right to be untouched?

It exists only in a surrounding supportive of the inclusion of an over-a-knoll, valley-like over-a-knoll.

The skill's working-into-the-Marrow's-dough's has not been digested, though its finished form has been tasted. Has the phrasal structure of a fugue subject's constant been mirrored so it can mirror? Has the phrasal structure of an over-a-knoll's constant been mirrored so it can mirror the mirrored? The undigested shape of the Marrow's comprehensibility has not reached its valley's top, though its *finished* form has reached reaching for itself.

It exists only in a surrounding supportive of the inclusion of an over-a-knoll, valley-like over-a-knoll.

To what extent does the phrasal structure of the Marrow bread have the right to remain uncut?

It exists only in a confine supportive of the kleptomania of a beyond, caesural beyond.

To what distance does the phrasal intertwining of a fugal misfortune have the right to be traveled?

On the eve of an *anniversary*, a celebration of a nova's nova, the lifting up of descent's a-dam, and an end put to the sound of a piano with no one playing, the ambulance was overbooked with the number of people
suffering from an overdose of that ancient stimulant known as the offspring of kola. How many will stay alive to witness their bang's drowning of the future's pooped-out Marrow bread?

Many have wondered as to what the credit given to the knife that was used in the cutting of the Marrow bread represented in terms of a carefully graded worth. Some claim that its scaling was a result of an inability to venture its anniversary as an object that will one day turn into a glorification of the day on which it is supposed to be glorified, an unaware pomposity of a zero-days-since anniversary. A sealed, stamped and sent letter has finally reached its destination.

How many will stay alive to witness their bang's drowning of the future's pooped-out Marrow bread?
On the eve of an *anniversary*, a celebration of a nova's nova, the lifting up of vulcanizations' a-dam, and an end put to the *sound* of a bottomless whirlpool, the ambulance drove, senselessly, to save the lives of the vulcanized, utterly solidified existences, volumes of undisputedly clear offspring of the undigested Marrow bread.

To what distance does the phrasal intertwining of a fugal misfortune have the right to be traveled?
It exists only in a confine supportive of the kleptomania of a beyond, caesural beyond.
To what extent does the phrasal structure of the Marrow's shed have the right to remain an anencephalic cabal? It exists only in a surrounding supportive of the inclusion of a soaked-in-vine, over-a-knoll's soaked-in-vine.

The undigested shape of the Marrow's aberration has reached its valley's *sober* land, though its finished form has not reached not reaching for itself. Is the *mirrored* a mirror used in mirroring the phrasal *bile* of the cake-like Marrow bread's taste? Is the *mirrored* a mirror used in mirroring the phrasal ache of the Marrow bread indigestion's *haste*? The ingredients of the Marrow's dough have finally been digested, though the pooped-out resultant has not been tasted.

It exists only in a surrounding supportive of the inclusion of a soaked-in-vine, over-a-knoll's soaked in vine. To what extent does the phrasal structure of the phrasal bile have the right to remain an anginal roofing tile? It exists only in encirclement supportive of the indigestion of a beyond, *caesural* beyond.
To what proximity can washed-away-into-the-valley's remains of its vine, be measured using a fugal shine?

The Art of Bird-Watching

I

Silky Fiber, Maybe

How riddling it is, the art of bird watching,
Its prohibition, a law there should be, is,
The literally interpretative of the high violence,
Yes, a vision blurred by a silky fiber,
That is the solver,
Maybe.

When its craft becomes needy of the *on-the-ground*,
Kaput a clog is, is that what the *what* and the *why* is,
The motive's definition, its *behind cajolery*,
Shoddiness buried, beneath the refinement's layer-infused?

How riddling it is, acclimatization in the desolate,
Blending in with the unripe used to be,
Acclivity's that which descents,
Its ripeness and unripe is calligraphy of the unripe.
Acclimatized is waiting to be wakened!

II

Abolitionism of the Contemplative

A particular fable's abolitionism of the contemplative:

Once upon a time of the *There was a white crow*,
Its *He flew with an utmost consistency*,
Prickled with *and therefore waited to be shot.*

A screaming of the *harmoniously screeching sound echoed.*
Its *The wound manifested as a bullet hole,*
Tempted the white crow to fall.
Prickled with *After long hours, the internal bleeding became external.*
He fell.

A particular fable's abolitionism of the contemplative:

The *on-the-ground* conversing, the between of the oneness,
Between a man with a big, white beard and a canal builder.
Its in between the "Is the white crow still walking?" and
"Both on land and in the air?"

A particular fable's abolitionism of the contemplative:

The callously abhorring-like of the superficially unaffected,
The using his in the that of a big, white beard's being cut off,
Its applied in the enigma of the improbable,
Without the pre-pause, found winging on the land,
Impossible.

The revelation in the form anti-nakedness *no more,*
The clothed seems to have been hiding the clothed,
The reality of the improbable, a corpse-like without the big, white beard,
The reality of the corpse-like with the big, white beard,
Impossible.

III

Silky Fiber, "Why is it white?" of "What would've been"

Questionability of the calisthenic as a law,
Of its lazily disciplinary in the taken down of a promotion,
Posited by the constructional of a Glass,
Answered the *on-the-ground vs. on-the-air's* elimination.

Rebel! Rebel!'s as a result of a barrier,
A translucent of the spherical's spherical,
Glass' prohibitive in the art of bird watching,
Created *on-the-air*'s conflict,
Its a Xeroxed of its anti.

Questionability of the burned down as a *Rebel!*,
Of its ashes in the created of a gigantic smoke,
Posited by the books' new form's white crow's curiosity aroused,
Answered the "What would've been."

The cacophonously screeching in a smoke's cadence,
Of its metamorphosis' black's resultant white's Xeroxed fell,
Posited by the attracted in the Glass' demolition's gunshot,
Answered the "A law there shouldn't be" of "Why is it white?"

The Art of Bird-Watching II:

Silky Fiber, "Why is it white?" of "What would've been"
(The Galactic Amphitheater)

Rebel! Rebel!'s of the white crow's *no more*,
Departed the Glass's, the conflict's *that is all,*
The second Glass's of the gunshot bullet's,
The revealed the amphitheatre's a whole.

The adoption of the bullet's unstoppable *faltering's,*
Of the circumnavigated triple's the spherical's,
Its filled the seats' galactic rows,
Copies of the man with a big, white beard's.

An outcast in the land of the asleep's,
Woke the galactic companions' eclipsed,
By having the bullet's run through his head,
Falling onto the surface of the widowed spherical's.

The decimating's had its transmitted to the eardrums,
The damaged's of the interested, seated friends.
It left a barren land from its the earthquake's,
The found their purpose in of the deaf's.

The Art of Bird-Watching III:

Silky Fiber, "The Deplaning" of "What has been"

When one of the bird-watchers, going out for a walk,
spotted a white crow in the sky
he got very excited.
But then, he looked more closely and realized
that it was a shiny airplane shaped to look like a white
crow.

He did not know what to think of it, this illusion,
why anyone would want to build an aircraft
that deceived so artfully. It wafted across the sky
like some subtle, refined odor that when sprayed
into the air, seemingly carried by a light wind,
if someone stepped in its way to be applied
to its lauded reputation, would prove to be
just that, a subtle, refined odor.

Out of this whiteness many other little, white dots
emerged, getting closer and closer,
they eventually made it clear that people dressed in white
were deplaned, or deplaned themselves, from the inside
of the white crow's replica, without the parachutes. One by
one they hit the ground, and the bird-watcher,
a chronic hypochondriac, hid in hopes to avoid being
hit.

It was very unusual. These people, each a couple of
inches sunk into the ground, still talked even though
their bodies, the broken bones sticking their sharp ends
in all directions, tearing through their skin, were beyond help.
They all asked to be helped up.

"If you want to know what the ubiety for bird-watchers
is I need you to help me out," one of them said. The bird-
watcher lifts him up.

"Now, while you are holding me, point my hand
toward the hole, making its palm face the sky."

The bird-watcher does exactly as he is told. The *white*
man then says "This is my imprint, the ubiety of the
art of bird watching. Feel free to try it out, to see if you
would fit."

The bird watcher tries it out and finds that not only
is it a perfect fit, but that he was a fool never to
have tried looking up at the sky, its inhabitants, by lying
down. All those years of incredible neck pain could have
been prevented if only he remembered that it was not
the only way. The strain had died away, but after seeing
an airplane made to imitate the white crow, the interest
had been lost.

On *Good* Intentions in the Place of *Bad*

The Prophecy of an Ancient Number X

There is going to be a clash,
A unification of *two* opposing,
Into a *singularity* of dabbing proportions.
An abracadabra-searching's entity.

The *two*, connected with an overhead's, vehicles,
One designated by the number 666,
The other set loose as 888,
Will collide in an apparently *two* opposing's,
Solidification-searching make.

The make's drivers' *depolarization*,
An event of efficacious violations,
Polarization of upon the sanctities of,
Will acquiesce, desecrate the desecrated's.

As the dented gets dented,
The *two* will decide to polarize,
As the third an over-head's triangulates,
The *two* will decide to be polarized.

Triangulation's the third an overhead's number…

None and everyone,
They will become an accompaniment,
A plain-song's undetectable abracadabra's,
An undetectable abracadabra's a plain-song.

Depolarized's polarized,
As the source of depolarization is not the depolarized,
They will bring the origin's to completion,
Beautify one another's that which they represent.

The source's fulfilled,
The *two* an overhead's' *two* anew,
And the second collision, contoured using the third an overhead's,
They will not end with *depolarized's polarized* attaining a knighthood.

As the *solidified* assumes the center-less,
The beautifying will realize its tooth's orifice,
Denuding the soldier-gentleman's and its pathos-imbued,
Making the way for the entrance into the tooth.

The internality of the internality,
Its represented by the flawlessly repugnant,
A result of the soldier and the gentleman stealing one another's,
Will realize its pointlessness with the *two* 888-666s of its entering's.

After the internality becomes symbolized by the externality of the externality,
After the inward's dent is molded into an outward's from the internal in horror,
The *two* will set their passengers adrift,
Admonish them of the acoustical nightmare of a decayed tooth's.

He, the knight on the black horse, will ride off population-less of the stacked-
on's.
He, the defender of the not-defendable, will ride the echoes of his horse's hoofs
into the,
The adjutant's, the illusion of the tooth's lowest being a freed ship's bilge.
He, the color-blind's creator-eliminator.
He, the lost calves' mother-"*caretaker*".
He.

They, the acrophobic dentist's driller's, will get an attack from the lowest's new
heights.
They, the *adulterated* descry's *death cell's?*, will turn black and white from the
eliminated's,
The color-blind's, the *vulnerable* to the bouncing of the clopping's eternal-seem-
ingly's.
They, the deaf from *an unaware* self-advertisement.
They, the lost "*caretaker's*" lost calves.
They.

The flying earwigs' crashing into the arrear's,
Will start looking for the stuffed's ears.
The losers of the echoes' duel's,
Will start looking for the victorious' mule's.

As the fainéant commences its ebbing's,
It will conjure up the eternal-seemingly's assassin's,
An inducer-speaker talking solely to the *"caretaker's,"*
An unnecessary tool used in getting the sedative out of the tooth-maker's.

It, the to-debouch-searching *scarcity-of,* is *"looking"* for the *fallow-less' to-cultivate.*
It, the to-rove-searching academy-of, is looking for the shaky-ground's to-devital-
ize,
To-vitalize, to-alight of the dismounted into the unstable grounds of the devital-
izing vitalization.
It, the *sun's only facular.*
It, the clay's only.
It.

The *fastidious* of the stealing-one-another's leader,
Will want to follow the echoes, the smoke,
Through the passage's the uppermost's dim,
Will have their imaginary is-detrimental, assassinated,
The dim's growing dimmer with the closing of the dim.

There the earwigs' residences,
Will realize the purpose of their home's temple,
The converting of a *harmless* decaying tooth,
into an *earnest* fang's true acoustical nightmare.

As the dimmer starts losing its sense of purpose,
As the knight starts stacking the earwigs' sculptures,
As the transformation starts its internal,
As the converting's intrinsic moves its from the bottom to the top.

As the inherent solidification starts its chase,
As the chased escapes its its, sets its echo free,
As the *two* adjacent break through the top's sealed,
As the *two*, the knight and its, start circling the newly formed pointed.

Triangulation's the third an overhead's number:
The *sun's only facular*, the 777, an ancient number X.

Perpetuity

The Chimera's Perpetuity

I
The Inquisition

The chimera looked at itself and thought
Now that I am a ghost, I can finally see,
clearly, that it is three different parts that
make me. But how did it come to this?
What does each part have to do with one another?

It started asking each part of its crumbly existence
what they had to say on this matter:

"I am a result of an asexual reproduction,"
said the chimera's number two, impatiently.

"Now don't be rude Mr. A. Let my number one,
Miss E., speak first!" *advised* the agitated chimera
its agitated head.

Number one did not seem to mind it, however,
and decided to postpone this little conflict for
a more appropriate occasion.

"That's all right. If he wants to say something
first, let him," the legs remarked passively.

Having heard this all-too-familiar voice on numerous
occasions in the past, the *adviser* and the *advised*
suddenly burst out into madness.

"Keep quiet, snobbish limbs!" exploded the chimera
and its head in chorus, like a pair of old chimes.

Realizing that a bad temper will not get it
anywhere, the monstrous appearance then decided that
an apology was in order.

"Legs, I am sorry. I am sure I speak for both of us
when I say that we completely lost it. It is just that
I...we have heard you talking in your messianic
voice too many times. Still, I am truly sorry."

At first, on the surface, the softening-up did not
seem to affect the head. Eventually, though, it decided to
say something of an *agreeable* nature.

"I suppose you are right. After all she is a
woman, and all women are snobs. They always, inevitably,
seek an opposite to their nature when in fact they shouldn't,
a suppression of the drive that has driven them at
one or another point to immorality. They're bright
enough to realize that immorality needs to be
avoided in order for humanity to reach morality,
for inhumanity to find its immorality.
They're bright enough to realize that
immorality shouldn't be suppressed, bright
enough to know that there is nothing wrong with
immorality, that pretending to be moral is what gave
birth to my being, a suppression of natural chaos as
a means of achieving unnatural chaos. Yes,
women are very bright, thus snobbery.
And those that ultimately end up following
a different path from that of a suppressive nature,
women that aren't snobs, are also snobs. For
they have to say to themselves, constantly,
that those women that are not them are,
thus snobbery."

Both the chimera and its legs looked puzzled,
as if not quite sure whether or not the *walking's*
should thank Mr. A. Finally, after a short silence,

the legs decided to share its feelings of uncertainty
with the rest of the company.

"A., I do not know whether I should be insulted or thankful."

Mr. A paused for a moment, giving himself enough time to
create his typical cynical-boy face, and then said:

"You won't disprove anything I've said if you thank
me. By not thanking me you will disprove nothing."

This made Miss E. slightly jittery. She
was trying very hard to think of something to say,
and then, as if it hit her right *between
the eyes*, she broke the third silence.

"But are you not a snob as well, having taken a side against
snobbery? Is not my great outcast and a famous preacher
in yours a snob as well? After all, he was so obsessed with the faith
and its preaching of the unprovable as the foundation of the
baseless that he fell into his own
trap, and thus ended up preaching
his belief in the elimination of the past's roots in order
to prove his ability of using aphorisms
for an inability to decipher them.
He became the snake biting its own tail that
he was giving speeches about, thus snobbery.
He ended up eating his whole self, leaving the head
alone and pretending that it was not alone, thus snobbery."

As the legs were approaching the end of its speech, everyone
noticed that something was not quite right. It would seem
that the head got so upset about not being able to change
the course of the conversation in its favor,
it wanted to break itself off. The *rest* of the body tried,
desperately, to persuade it otherwise.

"Head, don't do it! If you break off, not only will you
be unable to get anywhere, you'll destroy us as well!"

The exclamatory nature of this fragment had no affect on the
head, even though the sheer volume of it made it
nearly deaf. For when chimera had something to say,
all three parts of its body talked at the
same time, creating a sort of a double pair of chimes.
This irritated the head even more since it had to
talk when it did not want to.

Finally, the chimera found something to say that got
Mr. A. to be reasonable again.

"You know, head, I think it's safe to say that
snobbishness is unavoidable. The very fact that we
exist proves that there is no such thing as
natural humbleness."

This did not end the discussion,
but it did give the head a feeling of renewed self-esteem
that made it want to attack again with the old
self-assurance that it was known for.

"I think the real problem we have here is the fact
that the legs never were sure as to whether they
should be pleased with the partner that they got,
wondering whether she was beautiful enough to
find another, wealthier man."

Miss E. decided to *end* the conversation:

"Since the last time I found
something to say to what you said resulted in you wanting
to destroy us, I am not going to say anything."

"But I'm in complete control now, so please,
say what's on your mind."

"The real problem is not me, it is you. You are the one
who brought up the issue of women's snobbishness.
You are the one who as a result gave away
the inner complexes of a man who has a history
as a failure when it comes to women, a man who
had to create the image of woman as
something unlovable, something ultimately inferior.
Thus snobbery."

Mr. A., this time a successfully suppressed nature,
but still suppressed indeed, seemed to be calm, with
a slight tick to his eyelids.

"Of course what negates your statement is my never
saying that I wasn't a snob. I…"

The head was suddenly interrupted by an unfamiliar,
aggrieved voice. This voice may have been a stranger
to this conversation, but by no means was it a stranger.

"What about me? No one has asked me what I think
on this subject. After all, I am a result
of a sexual reproduction."

Mr. A. and Miss E. looked at one another with a
gossipy gaze, complete with the ever-ironical
touches, this time coming from both of them.
This new voice had its source in the form
of the chimera's number three, the hands, the stomach,
and all that was left besides the legs and the head.

"What is it that you'd like to share with us, Ae?"
asked Mr. A., fulfilling the *aroused* curiosity of
number three's *friends*.

"I am the ultimate goal, the cleanser of the past,
the perfect balance, the revolting conclusion,
a sheer ugliness that comes in two. I hate myself,
and yet the two of you love me. I am the only
possible reality that proves the reason behind
your ugliness."

The head and the legs looked at one
another once again, this time even more sure about their
attitudes. Again, Mr. A. spoke for both of them.

"We're so happy for you. It's too bad, though, that it has
nothing to do with what we are trying to
bring to a conclusion, even though it has now
devoured enough life out of our motivation
that we're very much going to conclude it."

"Well, at least I stopped something that
was going in circles, is and will."

II
In the Land of Ghosts

By the end of its inquisition the chimera
was nowhere even near to solving the
mystery behind its existence. It knew that
Mr. A., Miss E., and their offspring Ae, were the key
to releasing its agony into the looseness of the
heavy air that was keeping its unstable being
constantly replenished, but did not seem to be
replenished enough to have the right tool for
turning itself properly. Since the scope of its suffering was
immense enough to act as a successful incentive
to the imaginative aspect of its imaginatively
constructed existence's *mind*,
it all of a sudden realized that it never has

ventured beyond the surroundings of its residence,
in what must be the land of ghosts, a world filled
with victorious battles against *isolationism*.

The only obstacle that it was afraid of at this
point was itself. Will the three contrasting
sections of its structure agree
to this little adventure? The answers were as diverse as expected.

"No. Absolutely out of the question!" the unfeminine
voice of the feminine legs replied.

"Why not? After all, we have been sitting
in this starkly lit place long enough
to become a rottenly rotten aggregate.
The sky is the one of the night, and the land the one of
the day. What do you find so attractive about that?"

Strangely enough, the replied reply did not come
from the chimera. It was number two who found
the whole idea of a light without a source absurd,
a different motive from that of its aggregate,
but still, the positing of the same question.

"I cannot believe you do not find it just
a little romantic. You are truly inhuman,"
Miss E. started cutting off her sex.

Since it seemed like the solving of its problem was going to go nowhere,
the chimera decided that the only way to
create a clear picture of its hopelessness was to have a vote.
Miss E. was for it, Mr. A. against it,
and Ae was neutral. The chimera
was for it in the first place, and the problem was solved.
They got underway that very moment.

As soon as they reached a spot that was
about twenty meters away from their original
position, they intercepted something very strange,
something almost inconceivable: talking, little insects,
to be specific, beetles.

"Where are you going?" they asked, all talking at
the same time in a chorus that was somewhat like
that of the chimera's, except it carried much better.

Each say of the inferior, weaker ensemble reacted differently to this
situation. In the end, instead of giving away its destination,
it resolved to ask its slight interventionists to identify themselves.

"We are the death-watch beetles going-to-be.
Where are you going?"

"I never knew beetles could talk. And where are
your shadows?"

"We are the special kind, talking, without-shadows beetles.
Where are you going?"

"I...we are trying to find other ghosts
of chimeras. Do you know where we can look?

"This is the land of the inertia's law. We are heading
toward the far-off territory of the dead woods where the inertia
does not exist. It is quite possible that you will find more
of your kind there."

In order to make it more practical for the chimera to
be transported to this new heading, the bugs lined
up in a formal kind of a fashion, creating an apparent image
of a squared abyss with four even sides, in other words, a platform on
which the chimera was to stand on.

"Climb on!"

"But if we stand on top you, we are going to
squish the life out of you poor little things."

"First of all, we are not poor little things!
Second, we are indestructible. So indulge
yourself in what is supposed to be a preparatory
experience to what is going to come."

After the fable ended up obliging its potential transport's wishes,
the geometric collective really did turn out to be indestructible;
these tiny, little fragments of existences seemed to be able to hold anything.
They almost got a laugh out of chimera's thinking that they could ever be
crushed.
They did not understand that a gigantic monster gliding using little monsters was
somehow
not quite the happening in which a freshly made adventurer expected to find
itself.

The moment they finished pacing twenty more meters forward,
the strangeness of their now past complexity ceased to have any flavor.
Out of nowhere, a dark forest appeared without
any anticipatory signs. The monsters found themselves
in the middle of it, so it must have become
visible once its essence had become inhabited.

"This is it…we are here," the gliding bugs told their
companion. What they did not realize, though, was that
they were just about to hit something.

"Watch out! There is a tree in front of us!" warned
the chimera its platform.

The transport's eyes may have represented a completely different perspective
from that of its passenger, but this was not the reason
for their, in the end, being unable to prevent this crash. The invisible forest's
legend of being inertia-less turned out to be more than true.
Everything was gliding on the ground completely out of control.

Once our heroes encountered this tree,
they decided to hold onto it. The bugs' formation, unfortunately or
fortunately, could not prevent itself from being splattered, but on the other hand,
each one of them ended up with a dead tree to disintegrate,
or so it seemed.

"The utmost repulsiveness of the obliqueness of this land
is indescribable," remarked the panicked Miss E. An
obviously unnecessary statement when one takes into account
the "inverted" as a literal observation. The sky was
the one of the day, and the land the one of the night.

"This turned out to be a great idea,"
Mr. A burst out in joy-again, unnecessary,
but unpreventable.

Because Ae was not able to form any
relationship with its present situation,
it acted as a guide, a leader, and a rationalist
in these matters:

"It's so enigmatic, this land. Does it not
spark your curiosity that
the leaves, the dirt, and the rest of the
things to be found on the ground must
be gliding to somewhere? Where are
they all gliding to?"

Its parents were so taken by the processing of their *new* memory,
they registered nothing Ae uttered.
All they could do was have a subtle duel between their
not-so-subtle opinions. Especially the legs was the one that could not
calm down:

"The function of this forest may have aggrandized
it, but the essence of it certainly has not."

These words, along with number three's heart
of an explorer led to chimera's asking the
death-watch beetles what it should do.

"How do we know? Are you not thankful
that we have led you this far...and now you want
to know where to go. Obviously, the most natural
thing to do would be to go on going in the direction of
the west. It's your choice, and you better choose fast...
you've upset us, and when we are upset the volume
of the sound of our ticking usually reaches the deafening
level."

The most natural thing for the chimera was, in fact,
not going in one direction, but having a desire to fulfill three
different paths, the one of the west, the one of the north, and
the one of the tree that it was holding onto. If only it could separate
itself into three separate entities and solve its problem
right there. As it is, it ended up going in the
direction its broken platform advised it to go.

As they started heralding through the forest,
chivalrously, something unexpectedly heralded itself back at them.
The tree that they were holding on to was part of
the outer shell of the center of the forest,
not the inner. This spoiled their planning and timing that was going to
help them avoid the pleasantries of going deaf.
As a result, they were unable to escape
the beetles' ticking entirely.

Once they emerged from the forest, it took time for
them to have their hearing restored, just
as it takes a soldier time to recover from the sound of
an explosion that almost destroyed him.
In this case, the soldier that we are talking about, after
having fully recovered from its invisible
wound, had a chance to talk with maybe not
the whole person that threw

the explosive, but still, one side of it. This side came out of
the woods right after the chimera did.

"Aren't you suppose to be in there, with the rest of
your friends?" the mocking voice of the chimera
ascertained.

The lonely bug, with its head slanted downward,
answered in a broken voice: "I couldn't find
a tree to disintegrate. My brothers, they were all successful
in finding one, and of all of them, I had to be the one to be an
outcast. If only this part of the forest were visible, I could
find one right now."

"What do you mean by 'If only this part of the forest
were visible'?"

"This entire world is one
big forest, just like the one we came out
of a couple of moments ago. Where we are standing right now
is the invisible part that stays invisible, somewhat like
the first land of the inertia's law.
The fact that you weren't aware of this is the
greatest work of art you have ever produced."

"No, it's the greatest work of art you have
ever produced, you and your collective."

It stepped on the little fellow,
crushing it with great success.
A soldier without any facade intact except
the one of weakness is no soldier at all.

The new land that they found themselves in was
obliging the laws of inertia. However, it distinctly differed
from the one they came from. For the first time in the history of
their journey, the sky and the land were in perfect harmony.
They were both gray, a logical resolution to the previous two realities.

"Even though I hate myself, there is something in me
that inescapably corresponds to the image of an
indistinguishable horizon," the perfect balance remarked
about the perfect balance.

Miss E. and Mr. A were in a total disagreement with
their offspring, but there was finally an
agreement between them. The head told
its legs the legs deserved the after-pains, and the legs
agreed. The legs told its head that the head deserved
the after-pains. and the head agreed.

The chimera looked at itself and thought
Now I can finally look up at the sky.

It did. It was walking with its head slanted
upward, and then fell into the abyss
at the end of the world.

On Idealism's Communicators, Directly

Leech Plus Death Mask Equals...

The devotedness of the leech, was giving a speech.
The *now* eidetic, past's agrammatism-suffering *agister*,
had, it seems, no way of reversing the fading
of the bloodless face's natural paleness' naturalness,
its pre-death-mask's byword.
The devotedness of the leech, was giving a speech.

The *cabaletta's* of the plain's processed through the *not-so-plain*,
their the absence-of-the-inflection-perfection's dystrophic for,
had its audiences leave during the first third of its,
the face's blood sucked to extinction,
the decided not to be extinct.

The constructing of a red-colored death mask, completed the *deodorizing's* a task.
The teased audiences, after coming back in the second half,
now had, it seems, no way of distinguishing the idée fix
of the *dystopia*-causing's pre-pre-death-mask's,
stayed for the final act's dramatic representation of the leech's *sucking*.
The constructing of a red-colored death mask, completed the *deodorizing's* a task.

By mixing the superglue and the color, the audiences finally avenged themselves,
realizing the reality of watching the masked face of the mask-attached leech,
the leech that got lonely after having no more blood to suck in the second half,
the leech trying to break through the new barrier,
the leech that by attaching itself to the sticky mask enabled the audiences
to watch themselves with the help of the leech-attached death mask.

The aardwolf disguised as a leech *prevented* the termites from choking to kitsch.
The African mammal, after getting rid of the overpopulated world of termites,
revealed, it seems, the invisible mask's form of a bloodsucking worm,
explained the faulty futurology as the consequential's of the past's now's unclearest,
turned out the roof's barrier as not being flat after all,

as, indeed, something built out of four equilateral triangles.
The aardwolf disguised as a leech *prevented* the termites from choking to kitsch.

The conquerors fighting against the g"*a*"dflies' raids,
the g"*a*"dflies that are, indeed, very much the g"*a*"dflies,
the g"*a*"dflies that by being exterminated fulfilled their striving-for's
in the shape of a juvenile court without any judge other than an entity
consisting of the prosecuted and the prosecutor,
an entity that by assuming the position of an actuary as well,
advocate-less and jury-less,
achieved putting the matters of the insurance and the will
before the spotlight of itself.

As an iatrogenic, the out-of-the-boiling-waters entomophobic,
after diving into the pond-like of an uncharted character,
they provided, it seems, the *conflict* of two motives against three,
the leech-attached against the head-attached,
the attaching themselves to a leech and the getting out of the boiling waters
against the feeding itself, the *leaving* its, the making a zombie.
As the iatrogenic, the out-of-the-boiling-waters entomophobic.

The ibogaine's is not a result of an arson-like,
an eagle eye not lacking in the art of interpretation,
a lack of the inevitable naturalness of being inside so one can
eventually, and unconsciously, work toward the in-the-outside,
the ibogaine in the form of an inscription,
a revelation of one's under-the-roof as being
the holy tavern inside a holy tavern.

Hiding under the eaves, they eventually entered the grand, holy tavern of the to-
heave's,
the *ibogaine* as a dark hall of flickerings in front of a light,
reflections of the past, the present, and *the future*,
the *ibogaine* as the provider of an opium for the already addicted,
ibogaine, the hypsometer of the past.
Hiding under the eaves, they eventually entered the grand, holy tavern of the to-
heave's.

When they finished building their death mask, did they really,
finally realize that there was one constant found within the confines of their evolution,
the lung-attached leech?

The Record Keeper

The Figurehead's Log

Figurehead's log, mid-autumn:

Even though I am facing forward, I can
see everything that is happening on my ship.
The whole crew is working hard on cleaning
the entire upper deck, as if there is nothing
to be done inside. Lately, I have been
contemplating whether some
kind of a change should take place on this ship.
The crew looks exhausted to an extent where
they are just about ready to die, and yet they go on,
relentlessly, with their assigned task.

Figurehead's log, mid-winter:

It has been some time now since I
have been transformed. Thanks to this
new change, my crew has finally stopped
rubbing the deck. They look exhausted,
with some of them downright unhappy,
unhappy about wasting so much time on
such a banal task, unhappy about
the bad planning, their inability to even
try a descent into the inherent part of
this ship.

Figurehead's log, mid-spring:

I have finally gotten to being my old self
again. By the time the spring arrived
not only was the crew still tired,
they were also bored.
Right after I assumed my as of yet third form,
the first couple of days of March saw the crew
washing the upper deck even though it was

cleaner than ever before. The only conclusion
I could draw was that they got paranoid
after seeing me change without any change
on the deck that they were resting on.
They are still cleaning it.

In many ways, what has happened on this
ship may be a form of a demurrage. Ever
since the ship has been rented at the beginning
of the fall, and has not been returned on the date
agreed upon, around mid-fall, there has been an element
of unclear conscience in the air. On the other
hand, no one has tried to catch
us, so maybe the senselessness of guilt is
what drives this crew to the predominance
of an irrational behavior.

The Figurehead's Log II:

The Yacht's Log

Figurehead's log, mid-autumn:

Even though I am not facing forward,
I can see everything that is happening on my yacht,
and about.
Two men, holding hands, are seating on the stern
drinking cocktails, while our jet engine
appears to be performing…
We have just passed a ship, and to my sight,
its figurehead is an emulation of me,
with the exception of it being positioned to the fore.
We are now two oast houses, front to front.

Figurehead's log, mid-winter:

The ship that we encountered during the autumn
was now far behind, when, after a long conversation with my couple,
I have talked them into turning around to investigate.
Opposite to my situation, I found out,
from talking to "me,"
that its shipmates had no contact
with their "me."
The "me" was a negation of me, a "'me'"
as the kiln inside me.
We communicated regardless,
and its competitive apparition challenged me to
a race of a handicap class.

Figurehead's log, mid-spring:

That the chase between "me" and "'me'"
was handicapped there is no doubt. There is a mystery

surrounding "'me'," though, the mystery of
its deck being cleaned by every crewmember
available to it. "Who steered the wheel?"
a question that would have no significance
were it not for it being steered, spotlessly
(we encountered other ships in our path).
When we, I and my men, established that
the entire event bordered on boredom,
we determined to go around "'me'" as it went
on the straight path at its fullest.
Humorous though this may have been,
the reaction of anger that should have
come from "'me'" just did not.
Every time I, we, was starting a new
turn, I would ask "'me'," side to front,
"Who is steering "you"?"
The "'me'" never answered.
Arriving at the finishing line, they docked,
the yacht first, then the monster ship.
I, and a whole department of the police station,
arrested the yacht's two passengers,
then the monstrous crew of the runner-up.
The vessels did not have captains, yet
there were logs on both of them.

I had to arrest both crews for two reasons:
first, there was a discrepancy between the logs,
the monster ship's does not mention the yacht at all,
second, when we were wired a telegram about
who to arrest, the only information we had
was that the vessel's figurehead was a tobacco
oast house. There is a mystery about this arrest,
though, the mystery of our town's wires being
cut the moment the two ships docked.
Since we are out of the way from all the major
cities, we are currently looking for somebody
who practices the art of telegram.

On Happiness

The Hopping

"Hop, little rabbit, hop!
Don't stop to top.
Hop, hop, you anemic rabbit!
Don't make out of it a habit."

The rabbit is hopping, unhappily,
But has to hop to be a rabbit.
It can feel its current fragmentarily,
But can not sense the overdue as a slap-it.

"Hop, little rabbit, hop!
Yes, your heart did pop.
Hop, hop you heartless rabbit,
It was only the cooking alloy's inhabit."

It realizes the external membrane is still holding,
Starts hopping even more than before.
It adjourns the pectin-no-more molding,
Thinks there can only be a silence as a snore.

"Look! The juxtaposition may be exoterically-related,
The "*heartfelt*" and the *heartless* have mated.
Hop, hop you amnesiac rabbit!
Don't go hysterical, cohabit."

The insides of its heart have healed,
The snore-less sleep eventually achieved.
The two pasts between themselves created a shield,
The outer layer successfully peeled.

The Hopping II:

The Kangaroo's Confession

Kangaroo: I remember now. That was when I was hopping
in the middle of a desert with a little rabbit in my pocket.
I was hopping, and some kind of a barren door appeared
in the middle of nowhere, the kind of door that has
a window above it, and that as a result proved very useful when
one considers my nature of being a hopper.

What I could see through the window of this door was much simpler
than I expected. It was a continuation of the desert land:
in front and behind this door were two identical
realities. Still, I remember thinking how there was
something very lyrical about its design, like a lyrical text
set to nothingness.

Going through it was probably the worst thing I
could do, and yet, that is exactly what I did. Once on the
other side, my rabbit hopped out of my pocket, running
away with great efficiency. I was so desperate I fell into a
depression, losing completely my power of hopping.
While I was stuck, without any way of catching up with the escapee,
a miracle that I never expected to witness took place.

As a piece of perfect timing, my spirit left me, a spirit that
for some reason had no problem hopping, chasing the rabbit
without the tiniest bit of doubt about the outcome. I watched
the two of them hop, getting further and further, and the lack of
doubt slowly formed in me as well.

Kangaroo's Ghost: Unfortunately, we turned out to be complete fools.
You probably had no chance of seeing what happened, but in the end I failed,
miserably.

Little Rabbit: Did you? I don't seem to be able to recall not being captured.

Kangaroo's Ghost: You are not seriously trying to say that you don't
remember how you went right through my hands, how every time I caught up with
you I put my hands around you to lift you up into my pocket, and they turned out
to be no different than air. It must have been around four or five times I tried to detain
you in this fashion, four or five times I waged this senseless chase before we came to the
second door.

Little Rabbit: What door? I don't remember any door, my red friend.

Kangaroo's Ghost: The door that led to a green land, a place I couldn't enter,
and that as a result of your prolonged starvation represented pure heaven
to you. As a plains dweller I waited in front of it, hoping that you would at
some point come back, while you enjoyed the greens as if they were ambrosia.
Not only did you never return, the desert eventually became
a lush forest, and the second door became as purposeless as the first.

Little Rabbit: Strange how I remember none of it. I thought you caught me, and
that was the end of it. Are you sure I'm the one with memory problems? After all,
you don't know yourself, how could you
ever know what happened with yourself. Only wallabies live as plains dwellers,
and since you are most definitely red, and bigger than I am, there shouldn't have
been a problem with you following me through this second door that you men-
tioned. But then, you probably found that out once the second door became as
purposeless as the first.

On Poetry Relative to *Poetry*

The Acrostic of Triadic

The poem is figuring itself out.
Reciting itself, repeatedly,
it is finding its author unnervingly
frustrating.
Can he help?

"Maybe it's your past diagnosis,
maybe it still stands.
Maybe your suffering from agraphia
has an influence on your ability to
interpret others' works."

"Or maybe I have no purpose.
Maybe I am just a purposeless collection
of words that form the biggest nothing,
the ultimate in pretentiousness.
Indeed, if someone were to ask you
what I am about, what would you
tell them?"

"I would probably remark that
just like with the best of poetry, my
interpretation is not the only one.
On the other hand, you are one of my
simplest poems. It's so obvious
that you are about
juvenile delinquency, you are
probably the only one that
can't decipher you."

"What I find annoying are words
like 'lysozyme.' The entire me
talks about its nature and influence
on bacteria. What does that have to do
with juvenile delinquency?"

"It has everything to do with
juvenile delinquency. You're
about pre-nihilism, about what would
happen if the wall of its bacteria
were penetrated. Would there
be nihilism if we found out
what the essence of its "pre-"
were? That's what you are about."

"I understand. But why does it have
to be an analogy that uses a scientific
background?"

"Since the age of science
is closely linked with nihilism, and is
in many ways its representative, doesn't it
seem natural to present this unnaturalness
rooted in unnaturalness in an unnatural tone?
I'm using the analogy found within you because
I want to present pre-nihilism as the root of
nihilism, as its representative.
Maybe we should examine you once
again, just to clarify."

The author is reading the poem:

"Lysozyme's motive.

Alas, the lysozyme's motive would prove to be the den's friend.
Holy act would destroy all that is holy, and would mend.
Alas, the lysozyme's motive would prove to be the death's hand."

"Did you not say that I was supposed to be
an acrostic poem."

"Yes, I did."

"I fail to see what is so acrostic about me."

"That's probably because you're looking at the
ends of the lines. If you observe closely, you'll
discover that the beginnings reveal 'Aha,' in other
words, a phrase indicating a form of a realization."

"'Aha?'" But how can anyone know that it has
nothing to do with one of the systems used
for calling out the names of the notes in music,
for instance. Surely, you agree that it would
lend a whole new meaning to me, and that instead
of representing a realization of the ending as an
end at the beginning, it would represent three periods,
with the second being higher, and
going back to the original position of the first."

"In fact, that is the desired effect. For we can never
know whether it would end at the beginning."

"I find it a little preposterous, presenting such
a banal subject in such a subtle way."

"You may be right, but that's a whole different
subject."

"Why? I thought we were talking about pretentiousness.
Was I mistaken?"

"No, but we were talking about your pretentiousness,
not your race's pretentiousness. I think
we should end this conversation before
you start getting ideas about exterminating
your own kind."

"If I were to exterminate my race it would
be your fault, not mine. After all, your kind
created us. It is not my fault that I hate myself

to a level where I can no longer contain my anger."

The poet does not answer.

On Suppression, Directly

The Vaccine for Immorality

"...they drove before them a laden ass. 'What do these kings want in my kingdom?'"

Yes, but how did this ass become a separate entity?
Was it ever a separate entity?

The fable goes as follows:

Once upon a time, there was a huge vaccine constructed. Who constructed it, no one knows. Its purpose, it seemed, was to make a morality out of everything that was not. "Everything that was not" at that time included only a bottom, a bottom that apparently, somehow, did not quite agree with the rest of its body.

One day, the vaccine found itself in the hands of a stranger who decided that the contradiction needs to be evened out. This person took the giant needle, slammed it into the bottom, making sure that it penetrated its essence, and flooded it with morality. However, the stranger turned out to be not so bright, and should have thought before making such a harsh decision.

The desired effect of having the bottom oblige the laws of morality was achieved. A body that was an absolute pureness was not. As the anti-immorality entered this bottom, it also spread to the parts of its body that desired no change. All of a sudden, the body assumed the role of moral immorality vs. immoral morality. Its moral side of the past vanished because the two moralities, the morality of the needle and the morality of the bottomless, cancelled themselves out. A moral bottom and an immoral reason were all that was left.

As formerly stated, the giant needle was slammed into the bottom, something that may have to do with its future being contained within the boundaries of an endless suffering. It left a wound that would not heal, and that after about a millennium resulted not only in its death, but its companion's as well. The dead body was now walking, completely free of its past conflicts. It no longer had to worry about immorality or morality. Its burden had been finally lifted.

The Barrier, Whatever its Procedure May be, is Preordained

The Corrosive's

The nympholepsy had resulted in people put into bronze,
full-suit armors.
Their care for the out-of-their-reach had made them pyodermic.
The public occasions, family dinners, and children tucked into
beds by their guardians, their cloaked heads stroked with cloaked hands,
were now becoming unhandy in a quietly macabre-like manner.
Dying from an insufficient contact
and buried without being taken out of their disguises,
even each obelisk, be it a square or a cross,
achieved knighthood,
but as oppose to what they held,
were ordained in gold.

It was a law. You either wore it, or received treatment as an outcast.
Every armor had an insignia, giving a status to its wearer,
uselessness in the region of losers, and an impractical lawmaker.
The harsh punishments were present all the time,
and the most popular form of entertainment
was putting the criminals into the still-glowing,
slightly smaller than their size,
freshly made cloaks that melted everything inside them.
This division between the armored and the pyodermic was
very much like a section of the left part of a line dividing two quadrants of a semi-
circle
(one day to be a circle, maybe).

There were safety features that came with every armor,
that specified how to take care of it, and thus of oneself.
The most obvious threat was the rusting from an exposure to
too much water.

One day, a storm consisting of twisters and unremitting
amounts of rain reigned throughout the entire world.
Everyone hid in their homes that, eventually, found

themselves blown off one by one, and people flying in the air,
out of control, and crashing into one another.
After it was over, the lawbreakers were all dead,
and all that remained were citizens in their rusted
armors, lying helplessly on top of the wreckage,
totally paralyzed, their eyes moving about involuntarily,
violently, and their voices screaming from the agony of
being more than useless, regretting to be alive.

A father called his son helplessly,
hopelessly, without knowing that he was on the other
side of the globe. Many other senseless cry-outs
followed, and soon, they blended into one
chaotic weeping.

The screechy stroking had been deciphered.
Whether or not oily sprinkles are ever going to
fall from the sky was not.

The Humbleness and its Humblers

Rye-Bread Puppet

These short, swaying steps were taken by
one of our rye-bread puppets in sabots.
If you look closely you can see that some of the
stage's ground, a collection of upright nails,
still have the subtle residue,
a powder-like leftover that many have concluded is
there because the other rye-bread puppet,
the one controlling the strings,
did not walk its servant properly,
half-gliding the legs.

The plaque in front of the window says that
the difference between the servant and its master
was the way they were screwed
together. The master used real metal screws
for its joints, while the *servants* were matched
by the rest of their internal, chewy physique.
Never has there been any need to dispute
the roles of these two in relation to the third rye-bread puppet,
the one similar to the first but *without any strings.*
They were live puppets with a mission to let
the puppeteer be.

The play *without a play* progressed,
and the *puppeteer* decisively assumed
the role of the puppeteer.
It disconnected itself from its strings
and let the saboteur sabotage itself.
The puppet in the spotlight got tangled
and started cursing the third,
climbing the ladder of truth,
commencing a fistfight.
The *"puppeteer"* was eventually knocked out
and its tool disconnected itself from its strings,

using them on its prize,
and switching the roles.
Greed devoured the tool
and before throwing the second puppet
down onto the stage, it tied the third's
strings to it as well, attaching one
leg to a heavy object and finding both
the second and the third puppets on its stage.
The new puppeteer prevented itself from
joining them by putting the two crosses
at its end of the strings controlling the
second puppet under heavy weight as
well.

As these two new tools got up,
they found themselves supplied
with a series of holes.
The former *puppeteer,* since the ladder
had been removed,
panicked and ran,
to the left, to the right,
to the left, to the right,
always failingly,
stopped by its two crosses
being held by its puppeteer.
The counterpart to this event,
the third puppet,
there being nothing it could do,
walked passively off the stage
hoping to find some stairs.
After too much running,
the second puppet got a heart attack
and died, and out of boredom
the first climbed down
to the offstage to find the third.
Though the fall causes holes,
the sabots proved senseless.

There is a myth that the third puppet is
still looking for the stairs,
perhaps out of breath at this very
moment as we speak. If so, then
the first puppet is looking for it.

Someone stones the window,
enters its exhibited stage,
and starts chewing on the ancient
rye-bread puppet
like some starved rye-bread puppet.
Others soon follow,
and the exhibition becomes
interesting for a change.
They lose all of their teeth,
making the argument between the
propagator and the followers
a mumbling-like succession
of shouts.
"'Shame on you.'"
"'Why did you follow?'"

On Knowledge's Uterus

Vulvitis' Tzedakah

The obbligato, the vulvitis' tzedakah,
will attain itself like of a-deponent-in-an-
empty-court-of-law's, the before-the-vulva's.

The seduction, the byway's subtle selfishness,
will procure itself like of an-internally-capable's,
the storage-ready-to-explode-from-an-unending-*erectility*'s.

It is aglet's, it is shoelace's,
its spread-out's,
disentanglement's.
Which shoe?, which right-or-left?,
its first-third's,
entanglement's.

The slicing, its metal end,
the golden scissors,
its intercourse.
The growing-up, what love?,
the for-itself,
what mechanical?

What will?

What golden aglet's?,
the matching-separator's,
what seams?, the exploit-their-conscious.
Its colored blackness's's,
the three threads,
its differentiated, the *departmental*'s.

Gold-to-bronze's,
its will's-range's,

which ritualistic?, which mating?
Second-third's,
its feeding-itself's,
It is vulvitis', it is tzedakah.

The potentially-erectile-tissue-of-a-mindless (literally)-masculinity's,
will plant its seed *like* of a spoiled-participant-in-the-birth-of-ideas's,
the rear's filled, the excrements.

The body-with-a-sole-purpose-to-insert's, will disentangle-entangle
like of a the-three-threads-breaking-off-the-golden-aglet-at-the-opposite-end-to-
the-sliced's,
the vulva's cooling, the *naturalness.*

Vulvitis' Tzedakah II:

The Hysterectomy

It is likely ineluctable to think that hysterectomy is inexorable,
its removal of an entirety, the unsparingly alibiing act of storing
away a cubed alexandrite. A rubric's cube has a need, for a church service is a
complex matter, a Rubik's cube does not have a need, for a game for an accord
is a simple putter.

An alexandrite the size of a Rubik's cube did get *splintered* into many
little cubes, *pasted back*, made into a Rubik's cube, it had each of its
splinters assigned to a particular colored sticker of a Rubik's cube.

A duality-erased entirety's inside-outside-inside,
the refrigerated, sententious
akrosia of aligning, solving, the Rubik's cube,
its impalpable contact with its hard-to-please nature of,
after experiencing the satisfaction of a cheap intellectualism,
wanting to misalign what it has aligned so as to achieve
the *old-world's* chaos.

The unintelligibility systemized out of a need to earn the
pre-intelligibility achieved the *"old-world's"* chaos.
The dispraiser's memory that resulted in
new multifaceted faces did not prevent the stickers being
taken off, and the elastic bands' bursting.

The congruency's congruencies were *splintered* into congruencies
without a congruency, and were then glued back into a congruency *without*
congruencies, and became a duality-suffering congruency.

Inside-outside-inside-outside-inside.

On Rationality, Directly

What Is Abacus' Purpose?

An image of symbolic significance open to interpretation
was assembled on abacus' frame.
The question of its literality was interpretative too,
and the diversity of its spectators *led away from the former
potential's eventuation.*

In a math class, there can be those who belong,
those who do not belong, those who pretend to belong,
and those who pretend that they do not belong.
This particular instance saw its discussion surface
because it contained both the gigong-respecting pupils
and those opposed to its goals.

There was an immediate concreteness about the categorization;
the class contained the first and the last types of students mentioned above.
But before going on I feel that the image put under the augmentative forceful-
ness,
the abacus' formation, needs to be described as clearly as possible.

A straight line that gradually ascends, but at the same time continues,
reaching a peak, and then descends, connecting with the constant,
becoming one line that is the same length as the one before the ascent,
that's what it is. Now, we can go back to our math class.

As already mentioned, two kinds of students were seated in its reasonably
abhorring atmosphere of self-aware passiveness, self-aware non-submissiveness,
and their mediator. The identity of the womb of the reaching escalation
of the eruptive bloodiness that eventually connected its loose ends was surprising.

When I said that two kinds of students were seated in our class, I should
have added that the submissive ones would from time to time, in the middle
of the lesson, get up and perform their daily advocates, the gigong routines.
They were always ahead of the rest of their class anyhow; the teacher was on
their side.

The discussion aimed at the decoding of the abacus image's structural
to-what-it-yields was like an unstoppable dispute between the politicians and
the assassins. The politicians, their *agreeability,* would always
regulate their side's *publicities* calmly, intensely bringing out their
pressured pressures. The assassins, on the other hand, were beyond
a belief that the inner sphere of a human being, in their opinion cleanliness
as an impossibility, compressed into a squared box was rational.

The ascent and the descent, the line, these were all happenings that had
geometrical attributes sourced in formulas, calculations that in
accordance to the extent of psychological development were seen as either
the end, a means of reaching its practical appliance, or as having a
layer that visually, apart from communicating the need for its *angular*
decipherment, also on the pure basis of its *direct*, free of any mathematical
fulfillment, had an aura of hymnological simplicity that through its symbolism
symbolized a greater hymn than that of a *squared circle*, an appraisal of a naked
one that stood before the squared box with the pride of a cynical smile.

The tool had to be modified; there is no question about that. The number of
beads slid onto each of its metal rods had to be changed. The very accumulation
of spherical objects experiencing a stabbing-through had an accomplishment
of *anti-verbatim* about it. The masochistic *tendencies* of an artist, an inner
contest between wanting to find another artistic *tendency* and soaking
oneself in the intoxicative power of being happily unhappy, enjoying loneliness'
productiveness, in other words, a contest also between an aware masochistic
tendency and an unaware one, this jagging selfishness of for-the-sake-of-being-
the-only-one-in-contact-with-the-abstracted-principles is probably the best way
to sculpt the bead's hole's *abstracted principle's* sculpture.

How it came to "jagging selfishness" ceasing as a figure of speech was, at least to
me,
of no surprise. The argument's progression, a pointillist painting, was on one
hand
contrived by an opinion that the before-the-ascent was an idealism-bowing *cul-
ture* whose
straightness could easily be divided into two parts, the first, an amorphous

prolegomenon, leading to the second, organizing itself into yet another amorphousness, a pretentious prolegomenon, and that with the help of science resulted, since the suppression had lasted for a long
time, in a destructive disappointment that disorganized all that had been nourished to
that point with such suddenness that the shock itself had added to the numbing effect.

The midpoint of the ascent sectionalized it into an insensibility that stood on a firm ground
and a one that lacked resoluteness under its feet. The peak, the anti-foundationalism, conjured
unconsciously as the perfect, and only, engenderer for the working-backward's descent
that is an exactness solely from the perspective of the points dividing the insensibility and the insensibility,
and the amorphousness and the amorphousness, was found by the anti-anti-foundationlists
to be an oscillation considering that underneath it the line that ascends also worked its
straightness all the way to the image's from-the-left-to-the-right finality. When the murkiness assured that there is a reason for this constant, that, indeed, within the boundaries of the equation of ugliness, it more than made sense, the *inactive* members of the class took their pencils and ritualistically penetrated their opposition's members' skulls. Appropriately, the math teacher took the report cards of the executed students, and failed them all.

The Penetration of it All

The Rubber Bullet

It hits you right between the eyes, and then, bounces off.
Like an albedo of a celestial object, of a planet, of a moon, of an
asteroid?

No, like that of a sun:

Two suns feeding off one another, like two vampires-fruitcakes on
a desolate planet living with a hopeless dream that they are suck-able.
The albedo's kickstand is going to be used: unknown.
The rubber bullet leaning on its kickstand, in the air, is going
to happen: unknown.

One vampire, one metachrosis, two vampires, two metachrosis?
Not quite.

The unclear labeling:

Every morning, a chameleon-like vampire takes, in secrecy,
its only friend's paintbrush and paints itself the color
of the paintbrush's owner. Since the naked vampire, naked
because it has no need for its paintbrush, because it isn't
chameleon-like, has only one way to live its hopeless dream,
only one way to sustain "vampire" as warm-hearted, it constantly forces
its friend to choke itself in the poisonous odors of its paints.
Has the nakedness lost all of its sense of smell?
And the precision of its eyes gone blind?

The extension of their madness is positively decadent considering
that both of them think that they are suffering from aldosteronism.

It hits you right between the eyes, and then, bounces off.
Like a participant in a mathematical perfection of bouncing off straight into one's gun's tube,
into one's starting point?

Yes, back and forth:

Two bouncers bouncing off one another, like two suns in a
desolate galaxy existing with a hopeless dream that they are bounce-able.
The albedo's kickstand is going to be used: not needed.
The rubber bullet leaning on its kickstand, in the air, is going
to happen: not needed.

One rubber bullet, one will, two rubber bullets, two wills?
Quite so.

The clear labeling:

Every morning, a chameleon-like vampire took, in secrecy,
its only friend's paintbrush and painted itself the color
of the paintbrush's owner. Every morning, until one morning,
as an act of self-preservation, it shifted the power play.

"You know that I paint myself in order to accommodate you,
you just pretend that you don't know. Well, from now on
things are going to change. You are going to be painted instead
of me every time I change my color, so that you match me and
not I you."

The bluff was called.

It hits you right between the eyes, and then, bounces off.
Like a rubber bullet hitting its target over and over again
until it finally penetrates it?

Yes.

How cheap.

978-0-595-35485-6
0-595-35485-8

Printed in the United States
32830LVS00006B/55-87

9 780595 354856